Rumi

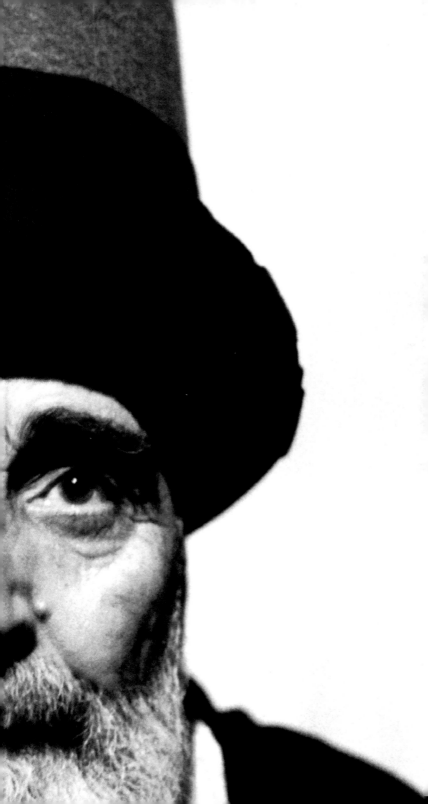

I am the slave of the Koran
While I still have life.
I am dust on the path of Muhammad,
The Chosen One.
If anyone interprets my words
In any other way,
I deplore that person,
And I deplore his words.

—*Rumi*

من بنده قرآنم اگر جان دارم

من خاک ره محمد مختارم

اگر نقل کند جز این کس از گفتارم

بیزارم ازو وازآن سخن بیزارم

Rumi
THE HIDDEN TREASURE

Shems Friedlander

FONS VITAE

This book is dedicated to
Sheikh Safer Muhib al-Jerrahi al-Halveti

Acknowledgments

I would like to thank
Dr. Maged Farag,
without whose generous support
this project on
Jalaluddin Rumi
could not have come to fruition.

This work was produced in honor
of the Istanbul Semà Group
and Hafiz Kani Karaca, performing
a *sema* for the first time in fifty years
in the newly restored Mevlevi Cairo *semahane*
in an effort of the
Italian-Egyptian Center for Restoration (CFPR),
under the direction of
Professor Giuseppe Fanfoni.

No presentation in English on the Mevlana Jalaluddin Rumi
could be done today without express gratitude for the quality
of scholarship and work of
Annemarie Schimmel and William C.Chittick.
One is also grateful to Reynold Nicholson
for his translation into English of the *Mathnawi*
and A.J. Arberry for his translations of the
Discourses and poetry of Rumi.

ISBN 1-887752-39-0

Library of Congress Control Number: 2001087452

Printed in China

Contents

Introduction

The knowledge of God is unimaginable to the minds of His creation. The infinite attributes of God are also within man, where they are finite. Thus the most generous person can never be as generous as God. Understanding this should eradicate spiritual egoism, which is one of the dangers on the road to God.

If all the trees on earth were pens, and if the ocean with seven oceans behind it were ink, the Words of God could not be written out to their end.
–Koran 31/27

The spiritual traveller can make a great journey while not moving in space. God has created the earth which is the coarsest of all things, yet when a seed is planted in this coarseness, such beauty grows from it. When the seed of love is planted in the earth of our body and we water and nourish it with the remembrance of God, we become the spiritual traveller who can fly above all things, walk on water, and make it rain.

The world is invisible to those whose eyes are closed. When the eyes of the heart are opened the hidden treasures of God are revealed. Others have preceded us as teachers. Past civilizations are teachers. The ruined cities, the dilapidated palaces

17

and decaying signs and relics of fallen empires and past nations can be examples for those of us who are here today. Surely we can see that the pains and pleasures of this mortal world are temporary, and that we will follow those who came before us as our children will trail us to the City of Mercy. If we do not learn from the lessons of others then our lives become lessons for others. The fourth caliph, Imam Ali, the son-in-law of the Prophet Muhammad, may peace and blessings be upon him, wrote in a letter of advice to his son: "The past and almost all that was in your possession during the past is not with you now. You may rationally come to the conclusion that the present and all that is in your possession will also leave you."

Umar, the second caliph, said: "The similitude of this world is that of a garment torn from end to end, but which remains attached by a thread at one extremity. That thread is almost broken."

This thread is the remainder of life for each of us. Its length is a secret, known only to God. The repetition of "There is no reality but God" is a polish for the heart, it is a satisfaction for the heart, it dissolves the hardening of attitudes which has caused a crust to form on the heart. It is like the ark of the Prophet Noah; whoever enters is saved.

The sedentary architecture of today's man has placed him in concrete blocks with rooms in the sky and he walks on an invented surface separated from the earth. The Arab nomads did not walk heavily on the earth. They built their homes gently, not to last longer than their needs, and they opposed all crystallization of the spirit.

On the Asian side of Istanbul, near the tomb of Akbaba, a fifteenth-century pious man, grows an ancient tree whose roots stretch above the ground like the fingers of a giant hand. A wooden bench encircles the tree and another bench faces the trunk. To the left of the tree is a cemetery whose stone markers reach to the top of the steep hill. In front of the tree is the old wooden mosque of Akbaba, and to its right at the bottom of the hill lies the village.

The bench by the tree offers a peaceful resting place. A crudely written sign, framed behind glass, hangs on the trunk of the tree. "Sit quietly in this place. Do not think or speak worldly thoughts. On one side of you is death, on the other is life. The mosque is in the middle. Contemplate this."

Breath passes out from the body but does not return. A breath which does not say His Name is a treasure lost.

Jalaluddin Rumi was allowed a portion of the knowledge of God. He was an ocean. If you place an empty glass into the ocean, what is in the glass is the ocean, yet it is not the ocean. This book is but a small portion of what is in the glass of he who was called Mevlana, our master.

The Roots of His Thought

We shall show them Our signs in the furthest horizons and in themselves.

Koran 41/53

The fish in the sea, although engulfed in water, does not see the water and does not know that he lives and breathes in water. We are like that fish. We fail to recognize that we have all these gifts and bounties which surround us and are in us.

The immense sky stretches above our heads without the support of pillars. The earth is like a carpet beneath our feet that gives us all the nourishment we need to live. The flowers, trees and plants are fed by a sun which shines on them and rain which falls upon them. A harmony exists which we are unable to see. Each fruit has a different taste and smell, each flower a different scent and color.

Animals were created for our use. Some we ride, we drink the milk of others, eat the meat of others, use their skin, horns and hoofs, some help us in our work. Each animal has a function and a characteristic which can reveal various traits within our own nature. A lion is not tied to the front of a cart. Just because we are dressed like human beings does not exempt us from having animal tendencies. There are men who appear as men on the outside but they are cobras who strike at whomever comes close to them. Others are like scorpions who sting. Some resemble peacocks, always primping and arrogant of their beauty. The sly fox, the meek sheep, the mouse who steals when no one is looking are characteristics and dangers that man can see in himself and learn from. Our mind is like a runaway horse that cannot be reined in.

God has hidden within each of us the knowledge of where we came from, where we are, and where we are going.

An ant decided to make the *hajj*, the pilgrimage to Makkah. Others said: "You will die on the road to God." Isn't this the state of us all? We are all going to the Mercy of God, whether we know it or not.

Jalaluddin Rumi understood the signs of God manifested in this cosmic harmony. As a mystical poet, a husband, father of two sons and a daughter, and a university professor, he drew on daily life for images to relate ideas. Rumi wove all aspects of life, from saurians and flowers to animals and prayer, into images of mystical poetry.

In the *Mathnawi* (Rumi's magnum opus which contains some 26,000 verses), Rumi tells us that prayer springs from God's presence in the heart and is answered even before it has been spoken. Rumi asks of God: "Teach us to pray," and "Thou hast given and taught this prayer: otherwise how could a rose garden grow out of the dust?"

His poetry reveals the highest secrets of prayer. "If you truly bow down in prayer," he said, "you cannot rise in your old self."

One bone-chilling winter, while preparing for the *Shebi Arus*, the Wedding Night when he would be united with his Beloved, Rumi spent an entire night in prayer in a small mosque on a hill overlooking Konya. We can almost see him on the carpet, in all his majesty, his head bowed in prayer and meditation, his woolen cloak wrapped about him to push away the dampness. He wept so profusely that his beard, wet by his tears, froze, causing icicles to paste it to the cold ground. In the morning his disciples found him still in deep meditation. Experiences like this one found their way into his words.

> At the time of evening prayer
> everyone spreads cloths and candles,
> But I dream of my Beloved,
> see, lamenting, grieved, His phantom.

My ablution is with weeping,
thus my prayer will be fiery,
And I burn the mosque's doorway
when my call to prayer strikes it.
Is the prayer of the drunken,
tell me, is this prayer valid?
For he does not know the timing
and is not aware of places.
Did I pray two full cycles?
Or is this perhaps the eighth one?
And which sura did I utter?
For I have no tongue to speak it.
At God's door—how could I knock now,
for I have no hand or heart now?
You have carried heart and hand, God!
Grant me safety, God forgive me.

Weeping is a step toward enlightenment. Joseph's shirt was brought to Jacob, who was blind from crying. He recognized the fragrance of Joseph on his shirt. Jacob also knew that his son was alive for if, as he was told, wolves had attacked him then his shirt would have been torn.

Fragrance is a word often used in Rumi's verses. Fragrance is the share of those who are deprived of the actual vision; it is a feeling of the presence of the Beloved.

I died a hundred times and I learned this:
Your fragrance came, and I was made alive.

> I gave my life a hundred times, and fell—
> I heard your call, and I was born again.
> I placed a net to catch the falcon Love
> Deep in my heart—he seized my heart,
> and went.

Love is the falcon that carries away the heart. When love appears, sleep disappears. God knows all languages and hears even the silent sigh of awe which emerges from the heart of a clement man. He who cannot fit into the entire universe can fit into the heart of a believer.

In the Koran it says "Call Me, and I shall answer" (40/62). He taught Adam and nothing else, neither angel nor animal, the names of created things, so that he could address and rule over them, for to know someone's name is to have power over him. And to human beings He taught the enigma of the Divine Names, that they may call upon Him, for He can be approached by His Most Beautiful Names.

> I was a hidden treasure
> And I wished to be known
> So I created man in order
> That I may be known.

Within this statement God reveals that He has given man the ability to know Him. To facilitate this possibility God has allowed man to know His Names. Here is one of the secrets of life.

The greatest gift of God is faith. Faith is a cloak which is always larger than its wearer, a cloak which never shrinks, but one which the wearer has to grow into. The process of fitting the cloak of faith is life. For those who can read, God has revealed His secrets in the Koran. For those who can see with the eyes of the heart, God has placed His treasures within His creation.

In the opening of the *Mathnawi* Rumi states:

> Listen to the reed how it tells a tale,
> complaining of separation
> Saying: "ever since I was parted from the
> reedbed, my lament has caused man
> and woman to moan...."

By the breath of man which is forced through holes cut into the heart of the reed, a plaintive, longing sound representing man's separation from his Creator is heard. The reed flute expresses a sonoral longing which is also expressed in a visual manner by the reed, split at its end and used as a pen to write Koranic verse, which is one form of remembrance used by many Sufis.

Hidden in the name of Adam, the first man, is another secret. The Arabic letters *alef, dal,* and *mim* represent man standing, bowing and prostrating in prayer. In the Arabic alphabet all letters come from the bending and reshaping of the *alef*.

"When the calligrapher's pen reaches the word

'Love,' it is bound to split upon itself," Rumi says.

The reed pen and the reed flute are cut from their source, they are fashioned by the hand of a believer, and both reveal an inner longing and love for God—one in honeyed melodies, and the other in beautiful letters.

Some fifty years before that frigid night of prayer in the mosque above Konya, Bahayuddin Veled, a prominent scholar and teacher, known as the Sultan of the Scholars, moved his family from a small village north of Balkh (present-day Tajikistan), to the city of Samarkand, an area where the cultures of Turkey and Persia met. His son Jalaluddin was five years old, and through his mother a descendent of Abu Bakr as-Siddiq, the first rightful caliph of the Prophet Muhammad. Bahayuddin remained in Samarkand some seven years, until the Mongol invasions in the area, which brought death and destruction to a large part of the Muslim world, caused him to take his family, friends, and students, some 300 in all, and caravan westward. Jalaluddin received his early education from his father and other scholars on the journey.

The year was 1219 and a decade of arduous winters would pass before the caravan finally settled in Konya, ancient Iconium, which was the capital of the Rum-Seljuk Empire. Here Bahayuddin, at eighty, was offered the esteemed position of university professor and taught until his death in 1231.

The caravan wandered from Iraq to Makkah and Madinah to Damascus and Aleppo, where young Jalaluddin studied Arabic poetry and history. At the time Aleppo was a place of concentration for dervishes and there is little doubt that this esteemed company would have come in contact with some of them.

When Bahayuddin stopped in Damascus he met Ibn Arabi, known as The Greatest Sheikh. As Bahayuddin and his son rose from the carpeted floor and turned to exit, Ibn Arabi said, "Observe, an ocean is following a river," alluding to Jalaluddin's future role as a spiritual teacher in the world.*

Damascus at the time of Bahayuddin's visit was, as opposed to the tension in Balkh, a prosperous, architecturally beautiful and religiously directed city.

It is related that earlier in their travels Rumi and his father met the Sufi poet Faridudin Attar in Nishapur. They sat together, spoke of passages from the Koran, and drank the customary tea. Attar presented young Jalaluddin with a copy of his *Asrarname*, the *Book of Mysteries*.

They journeyed north into Anatolia and settled in Larende, now Karaman, 100 kilometers east of Konya. Not all who began this expedition finished it. There was illness, birth, death, and marriage. Jalaluddin himself married in Karaman and

---

*The essence of this story is true, although some scholars attribute the incident as having occurred in the presence of Faridudin Attar.

fathered his eldest son, Sultan Veled, there. His mother, Mumina Hatun, and older brother, Muhammad Alauddin, passed on during the few years they spent in Karaman before moving on to Konya in 1228 at the invitation of Sultan Alauddin Kaykobad, who had constructed a splendrous mosque and religious colleges as an incentive to attract scholars to the region.

The sultan personally greeted them on their arrival to Konya and escorted them to the Altun-Aba Medrese, the school where the elderly Bahayuddin was to teach. Later they moved to a new *medrese,* where the lectures of Bahayuddin were collected and published in a book of three volumes entitled *Maarif.*

Konya is an area of arable land with frigid winters and deep snow, and is saturated with history. Konya was declared an Ottoman city by Sultan Mehmet in 1476. It remained under Ottoman rule until 1923, when Mustapha Kemal led a military revolution and made all of Turkey a republic. During Rumi's time Konya's inhabitants were mostly Muslims and Greek Christians; it was situated only a few days' camel journey from the Christian site of Cappadoccia, or Goreme.

After the death of his father Rumi, at age twenty-four, was given the university professorship. By now he was a scholar of theology and his knowledge and charisma attracted numerous students from Anatolia who acknowledged him as his father's spiritual heir.

A year after the death of Bahayuddin, one of his closest disciples, Burhanuddin Muhaqqiq, arrived in Konya. He had dreamt that his teacher came to him and said, "What are you doing here while my son is in Konya still requiring education?" Burhanuddin taught Jalaluddin the inner meanings of his father's work and familiarized him with the poetry of Sana'i, who had a profound influence on Rumi; reference to him or his work occasionally appears in Rumi's verses. Burhanuddin guided Jalaluddin in the *zahir*, exterior, and the *batin*, interior, of Sufi wisdom. He taught him various forms of the *zhikr*, remembrance of God, which all Sufi orders practice, and sent him more than once to study the Koran, Hadith, Islamic history, Arabic, and jurisprudence with masters in Damascus.

Rumi was influenced by his father's way of life and writings. In his *Maarif*, Bahayuddin states:

The most effective and strongest creation of God is love.

And:

Everyone lives in accordance with the amount he can perceive God. If he sees more, he lives more. He who sees God more learns more about the realities of sciences and religions.

Sultan Veled wrote of his grandfather:
"Men, women, or children, the young and the old turned to him when they heard him speak of the

inner mysteries and witnessed his miracles. When he died, a fire fell upon Konya. A grief burned slaves and free men alike. Scholars and officers led the funeral alongside the Sultan."

In 1240, after teaching Jalaluddin for nine years, Burhanuddin departed from Konya and took up residence in Kayseri, where he died a few years later. Upon being informed of the death of his teacher, Rumi travelled to Kayseri, said the Sura al-Fatiha at his grave, gathered his books and papers and returned to Konya.

In 1204 Ibn Arabi, whom Shihabuddin Umar as-Suhrawardi referred to as The Ocean of Truth, came to Baghdad, where he stayed only twelve days. Here he collected the cloak left for him fifty years before by the Sufi teacher Sheikh Abdul Qadir Jilani.

After arriving in Konya, Ibn Arabi married the widowed mother of Sadruddin al-Qunawi, the grandson of the Sultan of Malatya. Ibn Arabi guided his stepson, who was on the Sufi path, further in the way of the Sufi before returning to Damascus, where he spent his last thirty years.

So it was through Sadruddin al-Qunawi, who was close friends with Rumi in Konya, that the line of Ibn Arabi, and thus Abdul Qadir Jilani, is linked to Jalaluddin Rumi and the Mevlevi. The line of knowledge meets the line of love.

Anatolia was in political crisis almost all of

Rumi's life, which possibly guided people of all faiths toward his circle in order to taste the honey of his counsel. But his words changed in depth and meaning after Jalaluddin met the wandering dervish, the king in a patched robe, a lover of Islam and the Prophet Muhammad, Shamsuddin of Tabriz, during the fringe of winter in 1244.

As Mevlana rode past the place of the sugar merchants Shamsuddin reached up and grabbed the reins of the horse. "Who," he asked, "was greater, Beyazid Bastami or the Prophet Muhammad?" Rumi replied, "The Prophet is the greater. Why speak of another?" Shams then asked, "Then how can the Prophet have said, 'We have not known Thee as Thou ought to be known,' while Beyazid said, 'Glory be to Me! How great am I.'"

The two succumbed to one another's arms and appeared as one being to the gathering crowd of students and merchants. The lover and the beloved emerged as one and went into *khalwat*, retreat, for several months.

Rumi later wrote:

"Once I was in love with books. I towered above other scholars and men of letters. When I met Shamsuddin, the one who handed me the wine of Divine Love, I became drunk and broke my pens. My ablution was performed in a torrent of tears...."

Jalaluddin was drawn into and surrounded by the

light of Shams, which expanded to include him.

As the sun moving, clouds behind him run,
All hearts attend thee, O Tabriz's sun!

Shams' life was cloaked in mystery. He appeared and disappeared. Some thought he was one of the *qalendari*, dervishes who travelled mostly alone from place to place, shunned possessions and always lived in the moment. Rumi saw the rose, while others only saw the thorns.

Rumi's family, friends, and students couldn't understand what magnetized these men for months at a time. They entered the place of retreat, sat knee to knee, repeated he Names of God, occupied themselves with *sohbet*, spiritual conversation, and soared above all worldly things in meditation and prayer. Heart close to heart, they became one being, the lover and the beloved merged into ecstasy. Shams told him that the secrets and the mysteries of the Prophet Muhammad were in his own heart. The silent space between their words was filled with Divine Love; the silent space enveloped even their words, eliminating all differences which divide mankind. Like a bunch of grapes crushed into juice, they became one.

Rumi, the serious scholar, was being transformed into a mystical poet who spoke of love. He was like a dark ruby before it is touched by light and its true nature revealed. A different energy ran through him as he now saw the signs of God on the horizon and in himself. Shams was the sun that brightened the dark night, the winter sun which was no lie.

The secret love, this love of Mevlana and Shams, or of the companions for the Prophet Muhammad, is a love which cannot be explained with words. Rumi wrote a hundred thousand verses and still said he could not explain this love.

Most love is for money, sex or position, but this is a love in which one expects nothing and is willing to give everything, even one's life. To understand this love one must live it. To look at Shams and Rumi and attempt to analyze this love from a position outside of it is impossible.

Shams opened the heart of Rumi, and Rumi became an eloquent tongue for Shams. Rumi wrote:

> Love is the only illness
> More agreeable than health.

The secret and security of this love lies in the fact that although many intelligent people attempt to interpret it, they cannot understand it; this love cannot be understood through analysis. This is also the protection of all deep spiritual matters, for although their surface can be seen, their purity, which is hidden, remains untouched.

No one, not even one's own family and friends, can understand this love. It was Rumi's son Alauddin and some of his own students who, out of jealousy, killed Shams.

Mansur Al-Hallaj, while in prison, wrote the story of the moth and the flame. The moth sees the light of the candle, feels the heat, and approaches the flame. The only moth that could explain the true nature of the flame is the one which has been consumed by the flame. Replications of the idea of being transformed in the flame of love and of the one who searches for the truth appear throughout Rumi's verses.

There is the story of the elephant and the blind men. Each man approaches the elephant and touches a part of him; one the trunk, the leg, tail, ear and back. According to the part touched they described the elephant. It is like a fan, a water spout, a pillar, a throne.

Mevlana takes this story from Sana'i and carries it further. It becomes a symbolic story of human beings attempting to describe God—for who is able to see Divine Truth in its entirety.

The Sufis often say that if you seek Him you will never find Him, but if you do not seek Him, He will never reveal Himself to you.

Prayer brings one close to God. But Love is an even more direct route. Mankind should have love for all of God's creation, not only people but also animals, plants and flowers. Each has its own purpose in this harmony. God can be loved through His creation.

A consciousness of community is a remedy for moral decay. Faith in God is an inoculation against the diseases of the world, especially loneliness.

Rumi said:

> The lover visible
> and the Beloved invisible—
> Who ever saw such a love
> in all the world?

Love transcends and transforms everything. It makes what is transparent apparent, as Mevlana states:

> Through Love all that is bitter
> becomes sweet,
> Through Love all that is copper
> becomes gold.
> Through Love all dregs will turn
> to purest wine;
> Through Love all pain becomes medicine.
> Through Love the dead become alive,
> Through Love the king becomes a slave.

Mevlana spoke poetry because he was poetry. His life teaching was an oral transmission of the signs on the horizon and in himself, which has always been the way of the Sufi. If one learns what is in the books, perhaps God will reveal the knowledge that is not in books.

In Rumi's allegory the Caliph questions Layla, "Are you the one to whom Madjnun was so attracted and hence led astray? You are not more beautiful than other fair ones." "Be silent," Layla replied, "since you are not Madjnun." Whoever is awake to the material world is asleep to the inner spiritual world; his wakefulness is worse than sleep. The world is a book whose meaning changes with the understanding of the reader.

Rumi wrote:

> The *sema* is peace for the souls
> of the living;
> The one who knows this,
> possesses peace in his heart.
> The one who wants to be awakened
> Is the one who sleeps in the middle
> of the garden.
> But for the one who sleeps in prison,
> To be awakened is only a nuisance.

If you place an empty glass in the ocean, what is in the glass is the ocean but it is also not the ocean. In this double meaning lies the essence of Rumi's poems.

"My poetry resembles Egyptian bread," Rumi said. "When a night passes over it you cannot eat it anymore. Eat it at this point when it is fresh, before dust settles upon it."

He often refers to the words of Mansur al-Hallaj, who said that death is the real union between lover and Beloved. Mevlana wrote:

> I am a bird of the heavenly garden,
> I belong not to the earthly sphere.
> They have made for two or three days,
> A cage of my body.

Rumi constantly, by using the signs put onto the horizon, allows man to see his misunderstanding in relying upon a created being rather than on the Creator. In the *Mathnawi* he writes:

> He gave the cap, but Thou the head
> filled with intelligence.
> He gave the coat, but Thou the tall
> figure and stature.
> He gave me gold, but Thou the hand
> that counts gold;
> He gave me the beast for riding,
> but Thou the mind that rides it.

God says, "The human being is My secret and I am his secret." That secret is a light from the Divine Light of God. It is the center of the heart made from the finest matter. It is the sun of Tabriz. It is the Self which knows all the secret Truths.

Rumi says in the *Mathnawi*:

> The presence of a friend of God
> is a book, and even more.
> The book of the Sufi is not written
> With ink and letters, it is only a heart,
> White like snow.

An ancient Chinese text, *The Secret of the Golden Flower*, states:

> Whiter than snow
> More ethereal than ether
> Is the Self
> This Self am I.

It is the secret connection between the created one and his Creator. That secret does not love nor lean toward anything other than God.

There is a story in which the Prophet Moses was asked by God the different uses of his staff. "I use my staff to knock down leaves from trees so that my sheep can eat, and I use it to keep the sheep in line. Also, I lean on my staff." "Throw the staff to the ground," commanded God. Moses complied, and the staff turned into a snake. Moses jumped from the serpent. God ordered him to come back and pick up the snake. He did. The story could end at this point, with the lesson being that Moses obeyed his Lord even in the face of personal danger. But the essence of the story is that anything one leans on other than God could possibly turn into a snake.

Moses was then told to place his hand upon his heart. When he removed his hand the Name of God was written on his palm as a glowing light. The Light of God is in the heart, and all things which touch the heart will have light.

The Sufis are those who wish to throw themselves into light. One who does inner work becomes a candle which brings light into darkness. The one who does not perform inner work will be like a candle which burns down as it gives light

According to tradition, Hasan ibn 'Ali was once asked: "How is it that those people are most beautiful who pray at night?" He answered: "Because they are alone with the All Merciful, who covers them with light from His Light."

The guide became the follower. Rumi's students were agitated with their teacher's adoration of this stranger, this wild man of the road who had stolen the heart and attention of their beloved master and left them wanting what they once had. The atmosphere around them became intolerable, and Shams secretly departed Konya and travelled to Damascus. When the sun leaves it does not take with it what it has illuminated.

Rumi, in his longing, wrote:

The man of God is drunken without wine,

The man of God is full without roast meat,
The man of God is confused, distraught,
The man of God needs neither food nor
sleep.
The man of God: a king in dervish's frock,
The man of God: a treasure in the dust.
The man of God is not of air nor earth,
The man of God: of water not, nor fire.
The man of God, he is a boundless sea,
The man of God rains pearls without
a cloud.
The man of God has a hundred moons
and skies,
The man of God has a hundred radiant suns.
The man of God knows through the Truth
Divine,
The man of God is learned without books.
The man of God: no heresy, nor faith,
The man of God knows not of wrong or
right.
The man of God rode from Not-Being, look!
The man of God comes here in glorious
state.
The man of God is hidden, Shamsuddin!
The man of God: You seek and find him,
heart!

Rumi neglected his disciples for a time, as his
heart felt empty without Shams. When he heard that
Shams was in Damascus, Mevlana sent Sultan Veled

to implore him to return. Sultan Veled found him playing backgammon in the court of a caravansary on Salihiyye Mountain. He said nothing but pointed Shams' shoes toward Konya, indicating Mevlana's longing for his friend. Sultan Veled later wrote about this meeting:

"Shams began to speak and pearls came from his mouth. He sowed a new love in my heart and soul. He revealed secrets to me about the Koran and the Prophet Muhammad. He taught me to fly without wings. He unveiled my eyes so that I could see night as dawn. He took me to the boundless sea where I found inner peace. I experienced a feeling of freedom, like a bird no longer caged, and a safety and protection from every manner of danger."

They returned to Konya together in May of 1247. Shams, the wandering dervish, the light of lights, rode astride Sultan Veled's horse, and the son of the master walked at his side. Rumi likened Shams to an intoxication that increased one's self-respect, a meeting which convened in his heart.

Once again the jealous students of Mevlana found Shams to be an irritant and rebelled against him. They feared what they could not understand. Rumi's teaching touched their hearts, but Shams' words held deep hidden secrets that they found indecipherable. Shams wrote in his *Makalat*: "The microcosm is hidden in the creation of man and the macrocosm is the outer universe. But for the prophets the outer universe is the microcosm while the inner universe is the macrocosm."

When a heart beats in anger it is difficult to harness. An angry person is separated from his heart and in this state, having forgotten God, is capable of any act.

A group of students, among whom was Rumi's own son Alauddin, murdered Shams in dudgeon and threw his body down a well. Shams had disappeared again. No trace, no scent existed of his whereabouts. At first Rumi plunged into despair. Experiencing this separation, he then became overwhelmed by Divine Radiance and was transformed into a mystical poet.

"The proof of the sun [Shams] is the sun itself," wrote Rumi in the *Mathnawi*. "If you want the proof don't turn your face from the sun."

Aflaki relates that Mevlana was so distraught that he went into the garden alone and was not present at the funeral of his spiritual guide. They searched for the body of Shams for nearly a month. No trace. On the fortieth day Rumi ordered mourning robes of striped Arabian cloth, and replaced his white turban with a honey-colored fez made of camel's hair. He put on a shirt open at the chest, and rough sandals on his feet.

He then made a hexagonal guitar, saying:

"The six angles of this guitar explain the mystery of the six corners of the world; its string explains the hierarchy of spirits unto God."

There is a story from the American Indian tradition that after God arranged the six directions—East, South, West, North, above and below—one direction was still left to be placed: the most powerful of all, the one containing the greatest wisdom and strength, the one which led directly to Him. He looked to place this seventh, secret direction where it could not easily be found. It was finally hidden in the heart of man, for He knew it would be the last place that humans usually look.

Rumi wore his mourning clothes in the streets of Konya as if to announce the grief which bit into him like the ice of winter. On one occasion as he passed the goldsmith's shop owned by Salahuddin Zerkub, a close disciple of Burhanuddin, Rumi heard the beat of the small hammer as it flattened gold. As if overcome by a rhythm of joy which permeated his body, he began to whirl in ecstasy. The goldsmith encouraged his workers to continue hammering and soon joined Mevlana in the turn. Rumi had found an earthly replacement for Shams and he remained together with Salahuddin for ten years. Sultan Veled married the daughter of Salahuddin, ensuring the family ties.

Aflaki and Sultan Veled describe Salahuddin's

funeral as having music, singers, and ecstatic dancers, and it was surely a questionable event in the eyes of the Muslims of Konya. According to the will of Salahuddin no one was allowed to shed tears, for he believed that death was only a meeting with the Beloved which one should go towards smiling and happy. Perhaps this wish for dry eyes was complied with, but Rumi expressed the sorrow of his separation from his friend Salahuddin by saying in his *Divan* that "the sky and the earth, the intellect and the soul, have begun to cry."

Husamuddin Hasan Chelebi was a learned man, a poet and author who resided in Konya and became Rumi's immediate disciple and inspiration. He encouraged Rumi to write a work which would equal those of his poetic predecessors and soothe the hearts of the lovers of God. Mevlana, in 1256, began reciting the *Mathnawi*, in which he pays tribute to the one who wrote down the verses he spoke.

"O Ziya al-Haq Husamuddin, you are he through whose light the *Mathnawi* has exceeded the light of the moon. O you in whom all hopes are placed, your high endeavor is drawing this work God knows to where."

The two would sit up through the night, with Rumi reciting verses and Husamuddin writing them down and reading them back to his teacher. There was an interim of silence for two years after the completion of the first volume because Husamuddin was distraught over the death of his wife.

Most of his verses were spoken in the last twenty-five years of Rumi's life. He read the Koran, prayed and fasted, and sometimes went to the hot springs in the area. The whole of nature, flowers, fruits, animals, birds, vegetables, meat, minerals, the seasons, rain, snow, sun and ice all appear in the mystical imagery of Mevlana's verses. The fragrance of fruit and flowers, the sound of thunder and snow find their way into his expression. He likened the condition of nature to the condition of the human being. Life was the eternal sea of God, where one can drown or swim or walk on water. One could learn to walk above all earthly things.

Every act begins with God. Observe the palms of the hands, where God has placed His Ninety-Nine Names. When the Kadiri Order of dervishes sit in their *zhikr* circle they hold their hands in such a way that the fingers of the left hand spell the Name of God in Arabic. The Mevlevis form the Name *Hu*, Him, when they bow.

Rumi was the paradigm of the life of a mystical teacher. Altered by mystical experience, he turned to share this with others.

Rumi's circle of listeners consisted of people of different natures and professions. Women were always present at his *sohbets*, spiritual conversations, and it was one of his granddaughters who spread his teaching throughout Anatolia.

Five volumes of the *Mathnawi* were finished, and during work on the sixth Rumi became ill and weak. His rest was uneasy and his body suffered dramatic changes in temperature. Kira Khatun, whom Rumi married after the death of his first wife, was constantly at his bedside, as was his son Sultan Veled. His friend Sheikh Sadruddin came to visit and pray for his health. Rumi remarked, "May God grant you health, for there has been left nothing but a thin skirt between the lover and the Beloved." Because of love everything fell from him but the Beloved.

Yunus Emre, the first mystical poet to write in the Turkish language, mentioned the passing of the elder poet:

> Fakih Ahmed, Kutb al-Din, Sultan
> Seyyid Nejmeddin.
> Mevlana Jalaluddin, the world's
> greatest pole [Qutub]: where
> are they all?

As he rested in this weakened state earthquakes shook Konya. Rumi japed with those visiting him and told them not to be afraid, for the earth was just hungry and would soon receive a fat morsel. Death, he said to them, was not a separation but a liberation. Do not look for me in the grave, he said, for I will be in the hearts of learned men.

Mevlana Jalaluddin Rumi died in Konya, on December 17, 1273. The evening sky burned red as men and women of various religions pressed through the swelling crowd to touch the green cloth that covered his coffin. Sadreddin al-Qunawi was to offer funeral prayers for Rumi but fainted when he saw angels and the Prophet Muhammad joining the funeral. The prayers were then offered by Husamuddin Chelebi. The day of Rumi's death has become known as the *Shebi Arus*, Wedding Night, the occasion when Rumi was finally united with his Beloved, God, in eternal life.

Several centuries later, on December 17th, thousands who have been touched by the words and ideas of Rumi converge under the Green Dome in Konya to praise Mevlana's magnitude and grasp at the hem of his wisdom. He wrote:

> I am neither from the East nor the West,
> No boundaries exist in my breast.

Rumi understood that the signs were on the horizon, but that the secrets were within oneself.

The Sema

The deep stillness of the moment was broken by the plaintive wail of a single reed flute. Slowly the dance master of the Mevlevi Order of dervishes began to turn, his right hand holding the lapel of his overcoat, his long white beard brushing his chest. Head bent and eyes lowered, he whirled in ecstasy within a circle of men who breathed out the Name of God from the very depths of their beings, in the privacy of the dervish prayer lodge, a 300-year-old wooden building secreted among Istanbul's winding cobblestone streets. In the cold winter night you could see the breath of the dervishes surrounding him as they chanted the phrase of unity, proclaiming that there is no reality but God. Repeating the phrase, they turned, first slowly and then rapidly, until at last they seemed a blur around the dance master.

These images have occurred for some 700 years as dervishes in black cloaks have performed a whirling dance in remembrance of their Creator.

Although it was Muhammad Jalaluddin Rumi who inspired the whirling dance, it was his son, Sultan Veled, who organized the Mevlevi brotherhood and created the *sema* that we know today. Over the years Ottoman sultans became disciples of dervish sheikhs; in the seven centuries after the death of Rumi more than 100 Mevlevi *tekkes*, dervish lodges, were built, many by members of the ruling family. Prior to 1925 there were five active Mevlevi *tekkes* in Istanbul. Today, two are standing: one in Uskudar, which is used as a mosque, and another in Galata, which has been turned into a Mevlevi museum where an occasional *sema* is performed.

When Turkey became a republic, the Mevlevi presence diminished. The Order moved from Konya to Aleppo in 1925, then to Damascus, and in 1929 the Mevlevi Order came to Cairo and settled in the area at the foot of the Citadel just below the Sultan Hassan Mosque. The *semahane* which sits within this Mevlevi complex has been perfectly restored through the combined efforts of Professor Guiseppe Fanfoni and the Italian-Egyptian Center for Professional Training in the Field of Restoration and Archaeology.

The floor of the Cairo *semahane* is circular, symbolizing the universe, where the planets rotate at various speeds. It reflects the cosmos, architecturally represented by the dome directly above the *semahane*.

The Cairo *semahane* also houses a huge original

work by the famous *hattat*, calligrapher, Aziz Efendi, who lived in the complex some seventy years ago. He had been invited by King Fouad to come to Cairo and script a Koran. Aziz Efendi remained in Cairo and began a school of calligraphy, where he also taught gilding and *ebru*, the art of marbling paper, which at that time was primarily used as endpapers for handwritten books. As a result of the efforts of Hattat Aziz Efendi, who was a member of both the Rifai and Mevlevi Orders, Cairo became influencial in the advancement of the art of calligraphy in the Arab world.

In 1953, Sadeddin Heper, music master of the Mevlevis, approached the Konya city government with a plan to help revive the Mevlevi Order in Turkey. He proposed introducing the *sema* as an annual program in honor of Jalaluddin Rumi. After much debate the Konya Tourism Association accepted the idea, hoping it would draw visitors to the area. By 1956 a full *sema* with complete dervish costume was performed. Thus a gate was opened that brought both curious travellers and lovers of Rumi pouring into Konya. The elderly Mevlevis were filled with joy, for since the closing of the dervish lodges in 1925, they had whirled only in secret gatherings.

The Konya Tourism Association and Sadeddin Heper, who was once *kudumzenbashi*, chief musician, in the Galata Mevlevihane (the dervish lodge in Istanbul), agreed that new *semazens*, dancers, would be trained. Ahmet Bican Kasaboglu, who had learned the Mevlevi turn at age 12 and entered the Mevlevi monastery at age 14, was chosen as the *semazenbashi*, dance master. Konya once again opened itself to Rumi and during the week of December 17th several *semas* are performed in honor of the Mevlevi tradition.

When the *tekkes* are closed then the hearts of the dervishes become *tekkes*. The Mevlevi dervishes no longer walk through the doors of the three-hundred-year-old wooden *tekkes* on a weekly basis and whirl barefoot on the polished wood floors of the *semahane*. But the essence of today's *sema* is much the same as it has been for hundreds of years.

Before entering the *semahane*, Hall of Celestial Sounds, the dervish performs ablutions. Then he proceeds to dress in the whirling costume unique to the Mevlevis. His attire is influened by the mourning clothes that Rumi wore after the death of Shams. The *sikke*, the tall honey-colored wool hat, represents the tombstone of man. The *tennure*, a long white skirt, represents one's shroud, and the *khirqa*, a black cloak with long, open sleeves, symbolizes the tomb. Beneath the cloak the turner wears a *dasta gul* (literally, a bouquet of roses), a white jacket, the right side of which is tied down while the left hangs open. Around his waist is wound a white cloth, the *elif-nemed*, about four fingers wide and two-and-a-half feet long. On his feet are ankle-high soft leather slippers.

The dervish keeps his *tennure* inside out. After performing ablutions, he sits on his knees facing the *qiblah*, the direction of the Ka'bah in Makkah, holding his *tennure* on his lap. He recites the Sura al-Ikhlas three times and the Sura al-Fatiha once, in honor of the spirit of Hazrat-i Pir Jalaluddin Rumi. Holding the *tennure* under the armpits, he kisses its neck and places his head through the collar and his arms through the sleeves. As he puts the garment on it is turned right side out. He then ties the *elif-nemed* around his waist and places his *khirqa* over his shoulders.

He is now prepared to enter the *semahane*, which should contain a *mihrab*, a niche indicating the direction of the Ka'bah. In front of the *mihrab* is the post of the sheikh (a sheepskin dyed red representing the sun), and in its vicinity is a calligraphy in praise of Rumi which says *Ya Hazrat-i Mevlana*. From the sheikh's post to the door is an invisible line on which one does not step.

At the door, the dervish locks his feet, right foot over left, bows his head in salutation, then slowly proceeds to his place, which is assigned by rank; the closest place to the sheikh goes to the highest-ranking dervish. After the *semazens* have all entered, the musicians enter and take their places according to their ranks. At this point the sheikh enters wearing his *destar*, the sheikh's hat, and *khirqa*. Behind and to the right of the sheikh walks the *semazenbashi*. They lock their feet, bow their heads and offer silent salutations to the dervishes. The dervishes bow and return the silent salutation. The sheikh comes to his post and the imam begins the *salat,* the ritual prayer. In the Mevlevi Order the sheikh does not serve as the imam, and every *tekke* has its own imam.

After the prayer and the recitation of the Fatiha, the dervishes all prostrate, kiss the ground, and stand. All but the sheikh remove their arms from the sleeves of their *khirqas* and return to their places. The sheikh faces the dervishes, sits on his knees on his post, and kisses the ground. The dervishes do the same. The sheikh then opens his hands, holding his fingers straight, his palms towards his face with the two little fingers touching one another, and recites the prayer of the post, which includes a recitation of the Mevlevi lineage. At the end of the prayer a *hafiz* chants the *naat-i sherif,* a poem praising the Prophet Muhammad, which is preceded by the words *Ya Hazrat-i Mevlana, haqq dost,* friend of the Truth. When Mevlana is mentioned all the dervishes bow their heads, and at the mention of the word *dost,* friend, they slowly raise their heads. The *naat* is listened to in silence with closed eyes and no emotional expression. At the conclusion of the *naat,* the *kudum,* kettle drum, is sounded, followed by a *ney taksim,* reed flute improvisation, in the *makam,* tonal relation, of whatever composition has been chosen.

Following the *taksim* the *peshrev*, instrumental music, begins with the sounding of the *kudum*. The dervishes prostrate, say aloud "Allah!" and slap the floor with their palms, indicating the day of Last Judgement and the bridge Sirat that is crossed to get from this world to Paradise, and stand. It is said that this bridge is as thin as a hair and as sharp as a razor. The musicians also stand, with the exception of the *kudum* and cymbal players.

At the beginning of the Sultan Veled walk the sheikh steps to the front of his post and lowers his head in salutation. All salute in a similar manner. He turns to the right and walks very slowly to the rhythm of the *peshrev*. He begins his walk with the right foot, pausing with the toes of the left foot behind, then brings the left foot next to the right and continues in this manner.

As the sheikh takes three steps, the dervish who is next in line stands in front of the post, feet locked and head lowered. He steps out with his right foot, not treading on the invisible line. As he brings his left foot up he turns outward, pivoting so as not to turn his back to the post. He locks his feet and waits until the next dervish in line is facing him. They raise their eyes, facing each other, each looking at the point between the other's eyebrows, contemplating the divine manifestation within themselves. Simultaneously they place their right hands on their hearts and bow. The first dervish turns and follows the sheikh, walking in the same manner.

All the dervishes bow to one another at the post in this manner and slowly walk behind the sheikh. When they reach the end of the floor opposite the post, they stop, bow, and step across the invisible line with the right foot. When the sheikh arrives at his post the *peshrev* ends. The *ney* begins an improvisation. As the sheikh stands on his post the *ney* stops and the singing of the *ayin* begins. All bow their heads in salutation.

The *semazens* grasp the collars of their *khirqas* in their right hands, kiss them, and pull them off their backs. Each shakes his *khirqa*, kisses it, then half turns and drops it in such a way that it falls folded over into thirds with the collar on top so that it is easy to pick up later. They then stand, crossing their arms right over left, fingers stretched, right hand holding the left shoulder and left hand holding the right shoulder. Their feet are locked, right over left. With the exception of the *semazenbashi,* who still wears his *khirqa*, they are all in their *tennures*.

The sheikh walks to the front of his post and bows his head. The dervishes also bow their heads. The *semazenbashi* places his arms into the sleeves of his *khirqa*, walks to the sheikh, stops to the left of the invisible line and lowers his head. The sheikh's hands are placed right over left. The *semazenbashi* bows and kisses the right hand of the sheikh as the sheikh lightly kisses his *sikke*. The *semazenbashi* stands aside so that the dervishes may approach the sheikh without interference. One by one the *semazens* kiss the sheikh's hand, step over the invisible line, take three steps and begin to turn. They take silent direction from the *semazenbashi*. If his foot is extended slightly beyond his black cloak, it is a signal for the *semazen* to begin his turn on the inside of the dance master as the outside is blocked to him. If the shoe is hidden, the *semazen* continues to walk past him and begins to unfold and turn on his outside.

As the musicians start to play and the chorus chants, all the dervishes begin to whirl, extending their arms with the right palm facing up and the left down. This allows the spiritual energy to flow from above, through the body and back out through the other palm to the earth. Their tall wool hats are pulled tightly over their ears. Like fledgling birds, they unfold and stretch out their arms as their long white *tennures* trace circles in the air. Their lips move rhythmically as they softly invoke the Name of God over and over again. As they turn the *semazenbashi* walks slowly among them, signaling with his eyes or position to correct their speed or posture. The sheikh stands at his post as the *semazens* turn counterclockwise, repeating their inaudible veneration of God. The *semazen* is bound for a state of annihilation through mystical intoxication. Often he sees the multiplicity in oneness and oneness in multiplicity. There is no pretense. He sheds tears without knowing.

When the music ceases the dervishes face the

sheikh's post, stopping so abruptly that their billowing skirts wrap around their legs as they bow. They lock their feet, turn their eyes upward without raising their heads, and close their eyes. This prevents them from feeling dizziness. Then they quickly walk to the end of the circle and stand lightly leaning on each other to prevent falling.

As the first part finishes, the sheikh, who had stepped to the back of his post, comes to the front, and lowering his head, inwardly makes this prayer:

"O you who whirl in the circle of love, Allah's blessings upon you! Allah's blessings upon your feelings and your intentions. May He lead you to the truth, which is the beginning."

He then steps back, stands on his post, and bows his head. All bow in return. The *semazenbashi* walks to his place and bows his head to the sheikh, as do all the *semazens*. A second round of turning begins, which is called the "first *selam*." At its conclusion the sheikh recites inwardly:

"O walkers on the path of love, may Allah give you total blessings and lift the veil from the eyes of your essence so that you see the secret of the center of the circle."

The third round, the second *selam*, begins in the same manner. At its end, as the sheikh salutes, he inwardly prays:

"O lovers, true ones, Allah's blessings upon you!

Your circle is complete, your souls are cleansed. Allah has led you close to Him, to the true level of closeness."

The fourth and final round, the third *selam*, begins. It differs from the others in that all the *semazens* whirl in the outer circle. The sheikh, holding the right side of his *khirqa* with his left hand at the level of his waist, and the collar of his *khirqa* with his right hand close to the right shoulder, and pulling slightly outward, walks to the center of the circle, called the *qutb*, and begins to slowly turn.

He represents the sun, the dervishes the planets turning around him in the solar system of Mevlana.

The sheikh whirls slowly along the invisible line as a single *ney* plays a distant wailing sound that leads him back to his post. When the sheikh arrives at his post, he bows, sits on the post, and kisses the ground. The turners sit, and their cloaks are put on them by those who chose not to turn in the last *selam*. All sit quietly and listen to the recitation of the Koran. The sheikh recites the Fatiha and then kisses his post. All the dervishes kiss the floor and rise. The sheikh then sounds a prayer to Mevlana and Shams.

The sheikh leaves his post and says, *assalamu alaykum*. All present bow their heads as the *semazenbashi* answers aloud, *Wa alaykum as-salamu wa rahmatullahi wa barakatuhu*, stretching out the last syllable, *Hu*, Him. This concludes the ceremony and the sheikh leads the dervishes from the *semahane*, stopping to bow opposite his post at the far side of the hall. Each dervish does the same.

They depart the Hall of Celestial Sounds and re-enter the world, their hearts having moved in enraptured flight and ecstasy in the cosmic dance of harmony.

The remembrance of Allah opens the door from the known to the unknown. It lifts the veils of limitations and allows one to enter the place of no boundaries.

There are three levels of *zhikrullah*. The remembrance of the ordinary man is called "verbal remembrance," and is performed audibly in public or silently in private.

The remembrance of the elite is known as the "remembrance of the heart," and is performed by the heart and tongue in unison.

The remembrance of the elite of the elite is performed by those who have inherited the mystery, and their hearts are not distracted from the remembrance of Allah. "Men whom neither trading or selling diverts from the Remembrance of God." Koran 24/37

Such remembrance is no longer an act of will, but is performed by the heart involuntarily. It is called "the remembrance of the child of the heart," the *walad al-qalb* and is done with the tongue still and the lips sealed, as the heart repeats Allah, Allah.

The outward of a thing is its illusion. The inward of a thing, its reality.

Mevlana said:

> You searched the whole world for life
> Yet in your own heart you will die.
> You were born in the blissful arms of union
> Yet alone you will die.
>
> You have fallen asleep by the edge of a lake
> and now you are thirsty.
> You sit on top of a treasure
> Yet in utter poverty you will die.

and:

> You've only been here a few days
> and you've become so friendly with life.
> I can't even talk about death anymore.
>
> You're on the journey home
> And your donkey has fallen asleep
> in the middle of the road!

The Gharib Sema is known to the Mevlevis as the Secret Sema, and only occasionally performed, rarely since the closing of the *tekkes* and the dispersement of energy. The Gharib Sema only commences after the regular *sema* has concluded.

Some of the older Mevlevi *dedes* felt the *sema* did not complete a deep inner fullfilment. When the sound of bare feet turning on smooth wood has ceased, when the *ney* has become silent and the last *Hu* has stopped reverberating in the *semahane*, when the doors are locked to all but the turners and the lights are dimmed, the Secret Sema begins.

The sweet scent of incense permeates the celestial hall as the Mevlevis file onto the floor one by one and begin a slow turn. They turn with *sikke*, the tall honey-colored hat, and *khirqa*, the black cloak which wraps around their body. Their arms are not spread wing-like as before, but held as the sheikh and as Mevlana before him, with the right hand holding the top of the *khirqa*, opened slightly, and the left holding the *khirqa* at the waist. This is the real *sema* of Mevlana.

They turn toward their hearts, slowly, eighteen times, the same number every *semazen* turns each morning in the *tekke* or in their home.

The white of their shirt collars and the highlights of their faces are revealed by the soft light as they turn in the mysterious space which is not contained by any boundaries.

No music is played and the only sound is the Name of Allah which is breathed out by each Mevlevi as he slowly turns toward God; for it is the breath which is a bridge between man and God.

The time when the Mevlevis lived in the *tekke* has passed. The *sema* revived through tourism was a transition that has led to a cultural exchange of the ideas of Mevlana. It is time to make the journey of the Self and abandon ignorance for knowledge, war for peace, and separation for brotherhood.

The Music
by Nezih Uzel and Shems Friedlander

It is not ordinary music,
this dervish music, it is music
you drink with your whole body,
your whole being,
and you live this music.

As Pir-O-Murshid Hazrat Inayat Khan, of the Chishti Sufi Order of India, and a master musician, so beautifully states: "When we pay attention to nature's music, we find that everything on the earth contributes to its harmony. The trees joyously wave their branches in rhythm with the wind; the sound of the sea; the murmuring of the breeze; the whistling of the wind through rocks, hills, and mountains; the flash of lightning and the crash of the thunder; the harmony of the sun and

63

moon; the movements of the sun and planets; the blooming of the flower and the fading of the leaf; the regular alternation of morning, evening, noon, and night. All reveal to the seer the music of nature."

Music through the ages has been referred to as "the celestial art," so it is with good reason that the *semahane* is the "Hall of Celestial Sounds," the sacred space where the dervish unfolds and opens towards the *baraka*, grace, of heaven.

Appearance is what is outside, *zahir*, while essence is the interior, *batin*, which is not seen by all. Rumi says:

> Appear as you are,
> Be as you appear.

Sacred music, although heard with the ear, is felt by the heart. The tone and rhythm touch the soul, which is why music and breath can heal both physical and spiritual ailments. The heartbeat of the mother resounds in the womb and for months is constantly heard by the developing child, who hears the sound and vibration as a repetition of the Name of God. This is why it is a comfort for the child to hear the Name of God whispered in its ears shortly after experiencing the pain of the birth canal. Whispering is merely the sound of words pushed out by breath.

As Inayat Khan says: "Music appeals to all of humanity because all that has been created had its origin in vibration, in sound. The most important sustaining element in the human body is breath. Breath is audible, and most audible in the voice.

"Within the body is a constant rhythm as experienced in the beating of the pulse and the movement of the heart. Breath permeates every part of the body."

Ismail Hakki, who in the early 18th century wrote a commentary on the *Mathnawi* and composed music, said in his *Book of Liberation* that those without purity cannot animate the hearts of people. Their voices lack warmth, and they can never uplift a soul. Just as food gives physical strength, the Divine Word gives moral strength, but without inspiration the words are empty. A man of virtue, he said, feels the harmony of the universe within his soul through music. As one listens, one concentrates on God.

The primary instruments in Mevlevi music are the voice; the *rebab*, an ancient Oriental three-stringed violin with a body made of a coconut shell; and the *ney*, a reed flute which symbolizes man separated from his Creator. Rhythm, voice, and melody work together in such a way as to create a monotonous sound which is the basis of Mevlevi music. Rhythm and voice must be connected during the flow, but basically they are independent. The rhythm instrument can create a music of its own just as the voice can. Melody unites them as an outer shell. This monotonous music takes the attention of men and guides it toward meditation. As one concentrates on the music, he becomes one with himself and new insights can be experienced. The purpose of the music is to increase wisdom. We don't have to enjoy the music, but it causes us to reflect. Mevlevi music is not for listening, it is for participation. The music, the dance, and oneness with Mevlana are essential to the ceremony. A missing element can spoil the sacredness and make the ceremony pointless. It makes little difference whether one plays this music or listens, for the music reflects the soul.

All music reflects the geographical area from which it originated. Mevlevi music echos the energy and enthusiasm of the Asian mountains as well as the dignity and serenity of the plains.

Mevlevi music is a part of Turkish religious music, which in turn is a part of Turkish classical music. Turkish religious music has two main branches. The first is the music of the mosque; the second is mystical music, of which Mevlevi music is a part. Mystical Mevlevi music has different styles within itself.

The music is generally directed by the chief drummer, *kudumzenbashi*, who is responsible for the flow of the music and decides whether it is to be played rapidly or slowly. The mystical atmosphere in the ceremony room influences his decision even though he himself dictates the relationship between the music and the dance. If the room is quiet and static, this is felt by the *kudumzenbashi*, and he will apply this influence to the music. It is important to note that the *kudumzenbashi* probably is not aware of being influenced because of his concentration on the ceremony. High concentration brings unawareness and thus spontaneity.

The *ney* players are directed by the *neyzenbashi*, who makes a long improvisation called a *taksim* at various points in the ceremony.

Most of the ceremony is oral. The words are the poetry of Rumi and other mystical poets. Dervish music cannot be written in notes. Notes do not include the soul of the dervish, they are only to remember the music. The earliest-known Mevlevi music dates back to the fourteenth century.

Besides the *ney* and the *rebab*, the other important instrument in the Mevlevi ceremony is the *kudum*, a small double drum used for rhythm and played with drumsticks.

The voice is used for the call to prayer, to relieve those who listen from the cares of the world, and the recitation of the Koran. Within the repetition of words lies a mystery. For example, the *tawhid*, the phrase of unity proclaiming that there is no reality but God, satisfies the heart of the one repeating the phrase. A glimpse of Truth is revealed by vibrations and sound.

As the Sufis say: *Hush der dem*, be present at every breath. Do not let your attention wander for the duration of a single breath.

Timetable

A historical linkage of people and events during the life of Jalaluddin Rumi

1207   Jalaluddin Rumi, Persian mystical poet,
       founder of the Whirling Dervishes, is born
1209   Francis of Assisi issues first rules of
       his brotherhood
1210   Ibn Arabi arrives in Konya (b. 1165, d.
       1240)
1211   Genghis Khan invades China
1212   Children's Crusade
1214   Peking captured by Genghis Khan
1215   Magna Carta signed
1218   Genghis Khan conquers Persia
1223   Mongols invade Russia
1225   Cotton manufactured in Spain
       –Birth of Thomas Aquinas (d. 1274),
       theologian and philosopher
1226   Francis of Assisi dies
1227   Genghis Khan dies; his empire is
       divided among his three sons
1229   Frederick II, crowned King of
       Jerusalem, signs treaty with the
       Sultan of Egypt
       –Fariduddin Attar, Persian poet ("The
       Conference of the Birds"), dies
1231- Cambridge University founded
1233- Coal mined for the first time in
       Newcastle, England

1235   Ibn al-Farid, Egyptian musical poet, dies
("Nazm as-Suluk," Order of the Progress)

1236   Arabs lose Cordoba to Castile
-Sultan Attamsh of the Delhi slave dynasty
is succeeded by his daughter
Raziy'yat-uddin, the first woman Muslim to
rule the Indian subcontinent, who rules
until assasinated by her Hindu followers
four years later

1237   Mongols conquer Russia, take Moscow

1240   Border fixed between England and Scotland
-Yunus Emre, Turkish poet, is born (d.
1320)

1244   Khwarazmi the Egyptian takes Jerusalem

1248   Ibn al-Baitar, writer on Arab
pharmacology, dies (b.1200)
-Hajji Bektash Veli, founder of the Bektashi
Order of Dervishes, is born (d.1337)

1249   Louis IX lands in Egypt
-University College, Oxford founded
-Roger Bacon, scientist, records the
existence of explosives

1250   The Saracens capture Louis IX

1251   Kublai Khan becomes Governor of China,
and in 1259 Mongol ruler (until 1294)

1253   Linen first manufactured in England

1254   Marco Polo, Venetian traveler, is born
(d.1324)

1257   Saudi (b.1184), the Persian poet who

lived for 107 years, wrote "The Fruit
Garden"

1258 Mongols take Baghdad and
overthrow caliphate
–Abu'l Hasan 'Ali ash-Shadhili, founder of
the Shadhili Order of Dervishes, dies

1260 Meister Eckhart, German preacher and
mystic, is born (d.1327)

1265 Dante Alighieri is born (d.1321)

1266 Giotto, Italian painter, is born (d.1337)

1271 Marco Polo journeys to China

1273 Jalaluddin Rumi, Persian mystical poet,
founder of the Whirling Dervishes, dies

Selected Bibliography

Rumi's Works

Mathnawi (*Mesnevi*, Turk.), 26,000 verses, translated into several languages.

Divan-i Shams-i Tabriz, 36,000 verses, mostly ending with the name of Shamsuddin as if it were he who wrote them.

Fihi Ma Fihi (*In It Is What Is In It*), known also as the *Discourses*; gathered by Sultan Veled.

Makatib, a collection of letters.

Majalis-i Sab'ah, prose consisting of lectures.

Aflaki, Shamsuddin. *Manaqib al-'arifin*. Ed. Tahsin Yazici. 2 vols. Ankara: Turk Tarih Kurumu, 1959-61.
 −*The Whirling Ecstasy*. Calif: Prophecy Pressworks, 1972.

Arberry, Arthur John. *The Ruba'iyat of Jalaluddin Rumi*. London: E. Walker, 1949.
 −*Mystical Poems of Rumi*. Chicago: University of Chicago Press, 1968.
 −*Discourses of Rumi*. London: John Murray, 1961.

Bruchac, Joseph, ed. *Native Wisdom*. HarperSanFrancisco, 1995.

Baha'uddin Walad. *Ma'arif*, 2nd ed. Ed. B. Furuzanfar, Tehran: 1974.

Chittick, William C. *The Sufi Path of Love*. Albany: SUNY Press, 1983.

Friedlander, Shems. *The Whirling Dervishes*, 2nd ed. Albany: SUNY Press, 1975, 1992.
 −*When You Hear Hoofbeats Think of a Zebra*. Calif: Mazda Press, 1987.

Golpinarli, Abdulbaki. *Mevlana Celaladdin*. Istanbul:

Varlik, 1952.

–*The Sema*, tr. Tosun Bayrak (private papers).

Imam Ali. *Nahjul Balagha*, tr. Seyyed Mohammed Askari Jafrey. Karachi.

Khan, Hazrat Inayat. *The Music of Life*. New Mexico: Omega, 1983.

Lifchez, Raymond, ed. *The Dervish Lodge*. Calif: University of California Press, 1992.

Meyerovitch, Eva. *Rumi and Sufism*. Calif: 1987.

Nasr, Seyyed Hossein. *Islamic Art and Spirituality*. Albany: SUNY Press, 1987.

Nicholson, Reynold Alleyne. *The Mathnawi of Jalaluddin Rumi*, tr. and commentary. 8 vols. London: Luzac, 1925-1940.

–*Rumi, Poet and Mystic*. London: Allen and Unwin, 1950.

–*Selected Poems from the Diwan-i Shams-i Tabriz*, tr. and ed. Cambridge: Cambridge University Press, 1898, repr. 1961.

Ozturk, Yashar Nuri. *The Eye of the Heart*, tr. Richard Blakney. Istanbul: Redhouse, 1988.

Rice, Cyprian. *The Persian Sufis*. London: 1969.

Schimmel, Annemarie. *The Triumphal Sun*. Albany: SUNY Press, 1993.

–*Mystical Dimensions of Islam*. Chapel Hill: University of North Carolina Press, 1975.

–*I Am Wind, You Are Fire*. Boston: Shambhala, 1992.

Thackston, W. M. Jr, tr. *Signs of the Unseen* (translation of Rumi's *Fihi Ma Fihi, In It Is What Is In It*). Vermont: Threshold, 1994.

Trimingham, J. Spencer. *The Sufi Orders of Islam*. Oxford: 1971.

Turkmen, Erkan. *The Essence of Rumi's Masnevi*. Konya: 1992.

This book was printed on
135gm Couche´ matte
Cover is 300gm Couche´ matte
Text was set in 12 pt Bodoni Book
Book design and photographs by
Shems Friedlander
Edited by Sarah Sullivan

CAPTIONS

Page 1: Bismillah

Page 2: Nineteenth-century posed photographs taken in the *tekke*, the dervish prayer lodge.

Page 4: Konya Sheikh Suleyman Loras. The perfect man, the complete man, lies within each of us.

Page 6: Mevlevis turn in Konya. The recollection of God makes the heart calm.

Page 8: The sheikh and the *semazenbashi*.

Page 10: A Mevlevi participates in the Halveti *zikr* in Istanbul.

Page 13: *Ya Hazrati Mevlana*, written in the shape of a *destar*, the Mevlevi sheikh's hat, by Hattat Hamid al-Amidi.

Page 15: The *semazenbashi* Ahmed Bican.

Page 16: Cairo *semahane*. Photograph by Giuseppe Fanfoni.

Page 20: Rumi said: "Why art thou slumber-bound, like clay the earth carressing? In movement shall be found the key to every blessing."

Page 21: Another version of *Ya Hazrati Mevlana*, written in the shape of a dervish hat.

Page 68: Mystical Mevlevi's music permeates the *semazens'* hearts.

Page 70: One loses one's self to find one's Self.

Pae 72: *Semazen* participates in Halveti *zikr*, Istanbul.

Page 74: The dervishes stop abruptly, face the post and bow

Page 76: After each of the *selams*, the *semazens* touch shoulders lightly so they do not get dizzy.

Page 78: Sheikh Selman Tuzun of Istanbul sits on the post.